CONTENTS

The Secretary of State for Education and Science publishes reports made available to him by Her Majesty's Inspectors following formal inspections of a range of educational institutions in England. Individual reports are followed up with local education authorities, and/or with others responsible in each case, by the Department of Education and Science. HM Inspectorate have also produced periodic reviews, incorporating information obtained through survey work and through individual visits as well as from published reports, under the title 'Education Observed'.

The present booklet draws mainly on evidence gained from visits in 1989–90 to primary and secondary schools to inspect the work of paid non-teaching staff. The Inspectors asked these staff to describe and comment upon their work, and also discussed their role with heads and teachers. The booklet summarises the findings of the inspection visits, highlights a number of key issues and provides five examples of good practice.

INTRODUCTION

The introduction of the National Curriculum has focussed attention on the potential benefits of deploying more, and better-trained, paid non-teaching staff in schools to support the work of teachers.

This review describes and evaluates some of the work undertaken by these staff in primary and secondary schools, and includes five case studies which illustrate good practice. The findings are largely based on HMI visits in 1989–90 to 100 primary schools and over 50 secondary schools. Information from several surveys, including a survey of library provision in six local education authorities (LEAs)[1], is also included.

Some reference is made to the use of voluntary helpers in primary schools.

1. *Library provision and use in 42 primary schools. Inspected September 1989–July 1990*, 1 November 1991. HMI Report 261/91/NS.

SUMMARY

- While non-teaching staff enable headteachers and teachers to fulfil their professional roles more effectively and efficiently, they do not substitute for qualified teachers by teaching. However, in the vast majority of primary and secondary schools the work of these staff is so valuable that important aspects of teaching and learning would be curtailed without their help.

- The hours and scope of duties undertaken by non-teaching staff vary considerably, from the one part-time clerical assistant in a small primary school to the wide range of these staff, including librarians, technicians and clerical and language assistants, who work in large secondary schools. Some undertake tasks for which special training is required; for example, as laboratory assistants. A growing number are well qualified for their roles.

- The 1988 Education Reform Act increased the scope for non-teaching staff to make a contribution, for example in managing aspects of the school budget under the Local Management of Schools (LMS). Most LEAs have provided training to enable bursars and clerical assistants to respond to LMS. A substantial majority of heads reported that this had benefited their schools.

- Nearly all schools under LMS had conducted, or were in the process of conducting, reviews of their staffing arrangements. As a consequence the work of many non-teaching staff had been closely evaluated, leading in some schools to better job descriptions and clearer definition of roles. LMS is enabling and encouraging schools to exercise greater choice in the range of work undertaken by non-teaching staff.

- Primary schools, in general, made much greater use than secondary schools of voluntary helpers such as parents. The number of such helpers in primary schools varied from one in a small school to 66 in the largest, but there were normally between five and 10 such volunteers, most of whom gave up to six hours of help per week.

- Non-teaching staff were used effectively in the majority of primary and secondary schools and almost all the heads wished that they could increase their hours.

- In about half the primary schools inspected between 1988 and 1991 total non-teaching staff support, including clerical staff, amounted to under 25 hours per week. These staff undertook such tasks as the preparation of teaching materials, so that primary teachers were able to use their restricted non-contact time more productively, for example in curriculum planning and in completing pupils' reports and records.

- While voluntary help was valuable it was subject to uncertainties; for example, the volunteers' time could not be guaranteed and they were rarely prepared to commit themselves to a routine that fully matched the needs of the school.

- In primary schools both non-teaching staff and voluntary helpers in the classroom were usually well briefed and supervised. Many helpfully undertook such tasks as hearing children read and assisting with practical work in science and technology. However, in a minority of cases the contribution of non-teaching staff and voluntary helpers was not well enough planned and on occasions there were more in the classroom than could be effectively supervised by the teacher.

- About half the secondary schools had sufficient science technicians and about three-fifths had sufficient technicians for craft, design and technology. However, many heads considered that the hours for library and clerical assistants were too short, and this was borne out by the inspections. In over half the secondary schools restrictions on use of the library were attributed, at least in part, to a shortage of non-teaching staff.

- Despite the valuable and widely appreciated contribution made by non-teachng staff, there remained scope for improvement in many schools. Perhaps the greatest constraint on their effectiveness was a limited perception on the part of schools, and of non-teaching staff themselves, of the extent to which they could provide support.

1. The majority of non-teaching staff work part-time, often for less than half the week. Many work only during term time and most are female. The proportion of teaching to non-teaching staff varies widely from authority to authority and often from school to school within the same authority. Hitherto primary schools have had little room for manoeuvre in the appointment of non-teaching staff and as a result many still have only clerical assistance. In contrast, secondary schools generally have a wider variety of non-teaching staff, including support in the school office, technicians for practical subjects, and sometimes general classroom assistants and clerical assistance in the library. In small schools, both primary and secondary, non-teaching staff have relatively few opportunities for achieving a degree of seniority through the supervision of others or for career development. For example, while the duties of bursar and school secretary were separate posts in some of the larger secondary schools, in most they were combined in a single post.

2. A significant change brought about by LMS is that schools, within the constraints of their budgets, now have greater freedom to determine for themselves the number of non-teaching staff they employ. Consequently, at the time of HMI's inspection many schools were considering whether current levels and categories of these staff were sufficient to meet their needs. A small number of secondary schools were considering phasing out their third deputy head post in order to employ more non-teaching staff, and many primary schools had already decided that their present allocation of secretarial hours would have to be increased to deal with the administration of LMS.

3. Many schools would benefit by having more non-teaching support. About half the 300 secondary schools inspected in 1988–89 had one science technician per three laboratories,

which was then HMI's criterion for adequacy of provision, and the criterion of one craft, design and technology technician per four workshops was met by about 60 per cent of secondary schools in 1989–90. In the survey of library provision in six LEAs (see introduction) fewer than half the schools inspected employed enough library assistants. Between 1988 and 1991 shortages of clerical support were noted in about a third of secondary school inspections. In about half the primary schools inspected during the same period total non-teaching staff support, including clerical and all other tasks, amounted to under 25 hours a week. The number of voluntary helpers in the sample of primary schools varied from one to as many as 66. Most primary schools were assisted by between five and 10 volunteers, each of whom had a commitment of between one and six hours a week. Other volunteers gave occasional help with particular activities.

4.   Qualifications of non-teaching staff varied considerably. Relatively few in primary schools were formally qualified; most primary school secretaries and clerical assistants had received little formal training within the education service except to prepare them for LMS. However, many had trained previously for other jobs and held qualifications in office practice and typing. A small number were graduates. Very few came to their posts with information technology or word processing skills; however, their role in the administration of LMS required the rapid acquisition of such skills as well as knowledge of budget management. Nursery assistants usually had the National Nursery Examination Board (NNEB) qualification. A handful of helpers, mainly voluntary, were qualified teachers. Few special needs and bilingual assistants had formal qualifications but they had acquired expertise through some form of induction and on-the-job training.

5.   In contrast to non-teaching staff in primary schools, many

of those in secondary schools held formal qualifications; for example, the majority of school secretaries held a qualification (though most secretarial assistants did not). An increasing number of librarians had been professionally trained, and technicians held one of a range of Business & Technician Education Council (BTEC), City and Guilds and graduate qualifications. On the other hand very few general classroom assistants had formal qualifications, though a small number were qualified as NNEB or held the Certificate of Qualification in Social Work (CQSW). Some foreign language assistants had qualified as teachers.

6.   The previous experience of non-teaching staff varied widely. In primary schools many women brought considerable experience to their posts; a good proportion had previously been secretaries and a few were qualified teachers not wishing to return to paid full-time employment. Some nursery assistants (NNEB) had experience of working with young children in other settings such as day nurseries. In secondary schools a number of bursars had served in the Armed Forces or worked in commerce. As has been stated, secretarial staff often had quite extensive experience of office work, and many technicians had worked in industry. Few non-teaching staff had previously undertaken training with school employment in mind, but the wealth of their skills and experience was generally highly valued by schools.

7.   With the exception of foreign language assistants, most of whom were recruited through the Central Bureaux for Educational Visits and Exchanges, non-teaching staff were usually recruited through an advertisement in the local press or by word of mouth through parents and others in the community. They generally found the work congenial and interestingly varied: they enjoyed working with children, teachers and other school staff. Many found it helpful to have a job which fitted

reasonably well with the hours of their own children at primary school. Schools had few problems in recruiting non-teaching staff except as a result of financial constraint.

8.   Most primary school secretaries commented that the additional demands of LMS were pressing hard on their time. Many had developed skills which elsewhere commanded higher salaries and better conditions of employment and this made the prospect of alternative and better-paid employment increasingly attractive. Few schools offered prospects for long-term career development, and most non-teaching staff who gained promotion did so by moving to jobs outside the education service or to other schools which offered a better salary.

Office staff

9.   Tasks undertaken by office staff in primary and secondary schools had much in common, though they differed in magnitude and detail.

Clerical staff in primary schools

10.   All the primary schools had at least one secretary or clerical assistant, although there were wide variations in the number of hours they worked, often unrelated to size of school. While some schools were generously provided with one or more full-time clerical assistants, others had a weekly allocation as low as six-and-a-half hours. Duties of the primary school secretary encompassed most of those undertaken by a wider range of personnel in the secondary school, the work including routine typing, completing a variety of returns, answering the telephone and filing, along with more demanding tasks such as assisting with the management of the school budget, ordering and stock control.

11.   In the many schools where secretaries and clerical assistants worked part-time some routine duties such as answering the telephone had to be undertaken in their absence by qualified teachers and often by the head. There was rarely cover for short-term absence of the school secretary and when she was away the head usually undertook her duties including such tasks as collecting dinner money.

12.   Primary heads attached great importance to the work of clerical staff because, in addition to their secretarial duties, many performed tasks of the kind undertaken by general classroom assistants, under the supervision of teachers, such as photocopying, recording radio and television broadcasts, and occasionally accompanying classes on educational visits.

Clerical staff in secondary schools

13. All the secondary schools had at least one secretary. Secretaries carried out a wide range of duties which included management of correspondence with the Department of Education and Science (DES), the LEA, examination boards and parents; preparation of school leavers' references, testimonials and Records of Achievement; maintenance of pupils' records; typing class lists and option lists; typing teaching materials such as worksheets and examination papers; operating the telephone switchboard; maintaining staff records; and typing staff references.

14. In addition to the school secretary the substantial majority of secondary schools had one or more clerical assistants. Typically they maintained records of attendance and class lists; received, checked and distributed resources to the various departments; prepared statistical returns under supervision; responded to various requests from staff and parents, for example to locate a pupil; responded to requests from individual pupils about such matters as lost property and medical procedures; and made arrangements for medical inspections and for visits of careers staff.

Bursar

15. A number of the larger secondary schools had appointed a bursar or senior administrative officer, whom many schools regarded as a member of the senior management team. Some bursars acted as senior member of the office staff with a particular brief for financial matters, and many were also line manager for all non-teaching staff. Bursars generally supervised these staff, arranged the maintenance and letting of the buildings, ensured the smooth functioning of the school office, maintained school accounts including LMS budgets, took up personnel matters with the LEA on behalf of teachers and

provided financial information to the school, to governors and the LEA.

16.   Some bursars carried out other duties such as managing the school diary, arranging cover for absent teachers, making returns to the LEA and DES and processing examination entries. Where there was no clerical assistant to deal with routine financial matters the bursar often placed orders, chased invoices and banked school monies. Many bursars were members of the governing body's financial working party.

Qualified nursery assistants (NNEB)

17.   Qualified nursery assistants follow a two-year NNEB course of training which equips them to give skilled support to teachers of young children. All the nursery classes and units had at least one nursery assistant, and a number of NNEBs worked in reception classes in infant schools.   Under the teacher's supervision they helped to plan the work of the class, prepared and maintained materials and equipment, mounted and displayed the children's work, organised the classroom, maintained contact with parents, supervised children and assisted them with a wide range of work.

18.   The nursery assistants typically worked alongside teachers and played an important part in facilitating group work. They assisted with groups undertaking activities such as baking, painting, modelling and science. They also helped with language and mathematics, heard children read and supervised the use of apparatus. They reported children's achievements to the teacher and many helped to keep records of the pupils' progress.

General classroom assistants

19. Most general classroom assistants were employed in primary schools and worked with pupils of infant age. A minority of schools allocated them exclusively to the reception class but usually they were shared between two or more classes in different age groups. Few general classroom assistants had received formal training and most were dependent on the teacher for guidance as they gradually built up experience in the classroom. Under the teacher's supervision they heard children read; worked with small groups of pupils in activities which included science, baking, needlework and art; organised resources for group work; and prepared and maintained materials and equipment. Some provided a service outside the classroom; for example, covering and repairing library and reading books. Such assistance relieved teachers of largely non-professional tasks so that they could use their time more effectively to teach the children.

20. General classroom assistants had little involvement in teachers' curriculum planning. Their roles were often both demanding and diffuse, and depended to a large degree on the priorities of the teachers whom they assisted. The best contribution was made by those who were given a clear remit and who were carefully guided and supervised by teachers who had a clear view of the support that non-teaching staff could provide. The most effective of these staff were those who were trained by teachers to support pupils' learning and who understood that they should not, generally, do for pupils what they should do for themselves.

Special needs assistants

21. Special needs assistants were of particular importance to

qualified teachers, especially where they helped pupils whose presence in mainstream education required additional support; for example, children who were physically handicapped. They were employed in about one-third of the primary schools and in a smaller proportion of secondary schools; the majority worked part-time for 10 hours per week or less. The nature of their task depended to a large extent upon the specific needs of the individual child, but most helped to sustain and improve the quality of interaction between pupil and teacher: they maintained records of the pupil's performance for assessment purposes and increased the child's participation in many aspects of work, often with a particular emphasis on speaking, listening, reading and writing. From time to time they met the educational psychologist and physiotherapist to discuss ways in which the child could be helped. They assisted with therapy including physiotherapy sessions, and carried out special programmes devised by professionals who advised on care of the child.

22.   In a few cases special needs assistants employed in special educational needs support units helped teachers to prepare teaching materials, and they carried out a limited amount of work with individuals or pairs of children under the teacher's direct supervision. Many tasks undertaken by the assistants were learned on the job, in part because the support needed by each child was closely related to his or her particular circumstances.

Bilingual assistants

23.   Bilingual assistants worked almost wholly in schools serving communities where many families spoke languages other than English at home. They improved the quality of communication between teachers and parents by acting as

interpreters, and by translating written information about the school into the pupils' mother-tongues. The assistants often worked with small groups in the classroom using children's home language as well as English; this helped to develop pupils' learning in English and, equally importantly, it enabled them to understand more quickly the work in other subjects such as mathematics and science. Bilingual assistants were employed, almost always part-time, in one-third of the sample of primary schools inspected. Their efforts often improved children's access to the National Curriculum.

Voluntary helpers

24. Parents, governors and other members of the community provided voluntary help in almost all primary schools. In many instances they made an important contribution to the effectiveness of the school through their regular weekly commitment. Voluntary helpers undertook, under teachers' supervision, virtually any practical task, including mounting and displaying children's work; hearing children read; supporting group activities such as baking, art and craft and story-writing; and helping to supervise swimming. They ran the school library, organised toy fairs and bookshops, helped with administrative tasks, assisted with extracurricular activities such as gardening, chess and drama, and repaired and maintained equipment and books. Volunteers often assisted with educational visits.

Technicians

25. Secondary schools employed a range of technicians most of whom had qualifications and expertise which enabled them to provide technical advice for pupils and, on occasion, teachers. Laboratory and information technology technicians supported

the teaching of science and craft, design and technology in a variety of ways. Typically, they provided practical equipment and materials when and where required; maintained, organised and managed resources; constructed and developed apparatus; ordered and controlled stock; and tested new practical procedures and equipment.

26. Information technology technicians maintained equipment, ensured the proper functioning of software, developed systems to support teaching in a variety of subject areas, devised new information technology programs and modified existing programs, advised pupils and staff on technical procedures and resource matters and controlled and ordered stock.

27. The scale on which audiovisual equipment was used in many secondary schools often necessitated the appointment of a technician to manage it. Typically the audiovisual technician produced printed materials to support both teaching and administration, usually from original copy produced by others; recorded broadcast radio and television programmes; maintained stocks of resource materials (including artefacts and written and recorded material) related to particular topics; managed audiovisual equipment; and maintained and controlled stock. The secondary audiovisual technician undertook many duties which in primary schools had to be managed by teachers or by the school secretary.

Librarians and library assistants

28. In the recent survey of library provision in six LEAs (see introduction) rather fewer than one-fifth of secondary schools employed professionally qualified librarians. The substantial majority of school libraries were still managed by teachers, almost half of whom had under two hours per week remission

from classroom teaching in which to undertake this duty. In primary schools a teacher usually oversaw the library, sometimes supported by unqualified non-teaching staff or unpaid volunteers. Where qualified librarians were employed to take responsibility for the library they usually demonstrated their considerable professional expertise. They contributed to formulating a library policy, managed the library resources which often included extensive audio and video recordings and audio-visual equipment, provided a reference service for pupils, instructed pupils in the use of the library and provided a broad range of advice to staff and pupils. Some library assistants performed routine tasks such as processing book acquisitions, maintaining records, supervising borrowing and returns, arranging displays and making up book collections.

Foreign language assistants

29. Foreign language assistants undertook a wide variety of activities which supported specialist teaching in secondary schools. They worked alongside foreign language teachers to enrich both speaking and listening, extended the range of teaching resources through providing authentic materials, provided oral practice sessions for individual pupils and small groups and assisted with extracurricular activities. They advised on correct pronunciation and accurate idiomatic use of the language, and often helped teachers to assess pupils' oral competence.

30. Non-teaching staff contributed most effectively where their potential was fully recognised and their duties were clearly defined. Bursars were most likely to have clear job descriptions and lines of accountability and most nursery assistants (NNEB) in primary schools had a job description. The extent to which other categories of non-teaching staff had job descriptions varied considerably, and job descriptions differed markedly in quality. Most of these staff developed an understanding of their role through working closely with, and under the guidance of, qualified teachers. Classroom assistants for children with special needs, and those who provided language support, usually understood their roles particularly well because they worked under close supervision and on clearly defined tasks.

31. The quality and availability of in-service training for non-teaching staff varied considerably. It was quite rare to find a school which analysed carefully its training needs, and even where schools had started some form of staff appraisal it was uncommon to find non-teaching staff included. Few funds were set aside by schools or local authorities for training them, though many LEAs provided valuable LMS training for heads and secretaries together. Almost all bursars, school secretaries and clerical assistants had had training in the use of computer-based systems for financial management, much of it limited to a few days but nevertheless largely effective. The training proved helpful for handling other data such as class lists and pupils' records.

32. Foreign language assistants were all foreign nationals and were normally appointed for one year. They usually took a short induction course at or near the beginning of their appointment. About half the librarians received some in-service training, usually provided by the schools library service and covering such matters as library administration, develop-

ment of pupils' study skills and links between the school libraries and curriculum planning. Technicians were given little in-service training, and there was virtually no provision for general classroom assistants, whose training was almost wholly provided by the teacher for whom they worked, as and when it was needed.

33. The substantial majority of non-teaching staff made a significant contribution and their work was highly valued by teachers. However, the effectiveness of many was constrained to a greater or lesser degree by factors which included a limited perception, on the part of the schools and these staff themselves, of their capabilities and potential; inadequate management and in particular the absence of a job description; a lack of formal or informal appraisal of performance; lack of in-service training; and a shortage of time to perform duties. Many primary school clerical staff had too little time in which to undertake a wide range of tasks which included writing and typing letters, dealing with files and answering the telephone; in their absence much of their uncompleted work was often taken over by the head.

34. Non-teaching staff assisted teachers in a wide variety of ways and they often contributed significantly to the quality of pupils' learning. They helped teachers by releasing them from routine tasks such as preparing the room for teaching, preparing and maintaining resources and offering advice on technical matters. This enabled teachers to spend more of their time on teaching.

35. Secretaries, clerical assistants and bursars undertook a mass of valuable but time-consuming routine administration. Many mastered new skills such as computerised accounting and data-handling, and assumed responsibility for handling LMS data while leaving managerial control in the hands of teachers. Non-teaching staff often relieved heads of routine work such as keeping accounts and making statistical returns. One secondary school, for example, delegated to an administrative assistant much responsibility previously assumed by the senior teacher as examinations secretary. This saved up to 200 teacher hours annually and was but one example of the contribution non-teaching staff made to improving the efficiency of qualified teachers. In both primary and secondary schools non-teaching staff such as secretarial staff and bursars reduced to a significant degree the amount of time which heads and other senior staff needed to spend on routine administration. This increased the amount of time that heads and others could spend in the classroom: teaching, supervising the work of other teachers and providing in-service training.

36. Teachers of the youngest children found the support of trained nursery assistants (NNEB) invaluable, especially with pupils at the early stages of learning to read and write. Non-teaching support enabled teachers to provide work that was better matched to the developing abilities of the children, to organise group work more effectively and to give more attention to the needs of individuals. In short, the teachers were able to

spend more time teaching. Qualified nursery assistants were almost always included in curriculum planning and staff meetings and great care was taken over their deployment.

37. General classroom assistants relieved teachers of many routine time-consuming tasks such as preparing and clearing away materials and equipment, and arranging furniture for group work. With the youngest children they supervised visits to the toilet, helped the children to put on protective overalls for painting, craftwork and water play, and kept a watchful eye on children engaged in outdoor activities. Many classroom assistants helped to supervise and sustain a complex variety of group work. Such support enabled the teacher to concentrate his or her attention on the business of teaching, assessment and recording.

38. The substantial majority of technicians in secondary schools brought to their post a degree of expertise which reinforced – and on occasion extended – the teachers' own knowledge and skills. Secondary science teachers who were supported by technicians taught a higher proportion of carefully focused, well resourced and interesting lessons. Technicians prepared materials and apparatus and, as a consequence, teachers were able to concentrate on the teaching. The effective organisation of teaching materials extended pupils' direct experience, increased the number of problem-solving activities and helped to improve the pace of work. Science technicians sometimes assisted the pupils directly, for example by supervising their use of electronic balances, checking their readings and recording of results. One teacher, faced with a particularly difficult class requiring strong control, was better able to achieve an orderly atmosphere and a sense of purpose knowing that the technician could be relied upon to organise and prepare the science equipment. In about 90 per cent of schools inspected the quality of support from science technicians was satisfactory or

better. In craft, design and technology the quality of pupils' work was often enhanced by the support of a technician. Audiovisual technicians saved teachers' time by undertaking routine tasks such as printing teaching materials. In one large secondary school it was estimated that the single audiovisual technician saved every teacher an average of 20 minutes a week.

39. To be fully effective the work of foreign language assistants necessitated careful planning and some in-service training from heads of department. However, the contribution of these assistants nearly always increased significantly the quality of pupils' learning, and time spent in training them was regarded as a good investment. Working with individuals and small groups, they often skilfully extended the scope of pupils' oral competence and this generated increasing confidence. They polished the performance of older, more advanced pupils by helping them with language usage, vocabulary and pronunciation. They helped both during and outside timetabled lessons, and often provided individual language tuition for sixth form pupils – tasks which teachers were sometimes hard pressed to undertake. During lessons the language assistants sometimes engaged in dramatised dialogues with the teacher and this, in turn, encouraged the active participation of pupils: on occasion they gave a short introductory talk to initiate new work, helping to create an atmosphere in which it was natural to use the foreign language. They helped teachers themselves by bringing them up to date with current language usage and familiarising them with cultural developments, and by assisting with teachers' assessment of pupils' linguistic competence and with preparation and provision of authentic materials.

40. Many primary school libraries were supervised by volunteers who attended the school for a few hours each week. These volunteers assisted teachers and pupils in ways that were

similar in many respects to those of librarians in secondary schools. They encouraged the use of both fiction and reference books; supported pupils who were carrying out research, and frequently directly helped pupils to acquire study skills which, in turn, helped them to pursue their own learning. Most qualified librarians used their professional skills to recommend books for acquisition and many prepared book collections to support and enhance pupils' learning.

41. Assistants for children with special needs helpfully undertook such tasks as preparing teaching materials and, perhaps more significantly, they heard pupils read and helped them with a wide range of other work. In many cases they helped teachers to provide fuller access to the National Curriculum.

42. Paid non-teaching staff are employed in greater numbers in secondary schools than in primary schools. Many functions performed by these staff in secondary schools are undertaken in primary schools by voluntary helpers, few of whom have formal qualifications or training for the work they do. With the progressive introduction of LMS opportunities will increase for heads and governors of primary schools to review the number and type of paid non-teaching staff they employ; there is every indication that more and better use of such staff could enhance the quality of the teachers' contribution to pupils' education.

43. Schools need to consider how non-teaching staff might best be used to free teachers from routine administrative tasks, helping them to give an even higher proportion of time to teaching and other professional duties. Preparation of non-teaching staff entails carefully defining the fine line between the need to support pupils' learning and doing for pupils what they should do for themselves. Some primary schools have yet to recognise this distinction as a matter to be addressed.

44. The importance of non-teaching staff is likely to increase, particularly in primary schools which are taking respons-ibility for managing delegated budgets and setting up informa-tion systems for recording and reporting pupils' progress. Many of the changes consequent upon the Education Reform Act require a higher degree of expertise among clerical staff and greater delegation of duties if heads are to cope effectively with the steadily mounting administrative load. New roles may also emerge for non-teaching staff; for example, supporting teachers as they carry out assessment arrangements at the end of Key Stages, and servicing governing bodies.

45. It is rare to find systematic appraisal of non-teaching staff matched to a programme of training provided either within or outside the school. The increase in numbers of these staff in

recent years and the widening scope of their work reinforce the need for their roles to be better defined and evaluated. Clear job descriptions, appraisal of performance and provision of suitable training need to be considered by heads and governors if the contribution of paid non-teaching staff is to be fully effective.

46. The National Curriculum and delegation of financial management to schools have increased the need for non-teaching staff. If they are deployed to best effect then both schools and pupils have much to gain.

Trained nursery assistants (NNEB)

47.   The 40-place nursery school serves an area close to the city centre. All but a few of the children attend part-time and about a third are from ethnic minority groups. The buildings consist of a large house and two hutted classrooms. The house provides a homely and welcoming atmosphere but the variety of small and separate teaching spaces makes it awkward for staff to organise and supervise the children's work.

48.   The staff comprises the head, two qualified teachers and three nursery assistants: two full-time and one part-time. The nursery assistants hold NNEB certificates and have experience with young children in hospital and in infant schools as well as nurseries. The full-time assistants are thoroughly familiar with the school and the locality, having worked here for nine and 12 years respectively. They join with teachers in visiting each child at home shortly before entry to school.

49.   There are two classes of 20 children, each with its own teacher and a full-time nursery assistant. The part-time nursery assistant shares her time equally between the two classes. The head teaches regularly in both classes.

50.   The staff work as a team to make maximum use of each others' interests, knowledge and skills. The role of the nursery assistants has evolved over the years and the standard job description provided by the LEA at the time of their appointment no longer fits their role; consequently the job description is being re-written. The nursery assistants are fully involved in planning children's work, and they regularly discuss with teachers routine activities such as painting and constructional play, and special themes which are to be introduced; for example, work on the theme 'New Life' included hatching ducks' eggs, rearing caterpillars, growing seeds and a visit to observe

young wildfowl on a near-by lake. At the planning stage the teams consider the educational purposes of each activity and the skills, knowledge and understanding which children are expected to acquire. Teachers check that the whole provision adds up to a well-balanced curriculum, and both teachers and nursery assistants contribute ideas and suggestions based on their personal knowledge, interests and experience. One nursery assistant, for example, takes a particular interest in art and craft.

51. Teachers and nursery assistants together organise the classrooms and make sure that there is enough equipment to implement their plans, and that it is suitably arranged in the right places. Help from the nursery assistants considerably reduces the amount of time which teachers have to spend on this task.

52. While children are at work, the nursery assistant helps the teacher by ensuring that group activities run smoothly. At the end of each session teacher and assistant briefly compare and record their observations, taking stock of what has been achieved and checking that all children have been systematically observed and guided. Decisions are taken, for example, about whether a particular child will benefit by persisting with an activity or should be encouraged to tackle something different. Such discussions inevitably sharpen the adults' perceptions of both purpose and progression in the children's learning, highlight individual needs and help to show where provision can be improved. The teachers, who are responsible for assessing and recording the children's progress, value this dialogue and insights contributed by the nursery assistants. Once a week the head provides a little non-contact time for the pair responsible for each class to complete the teacher's review, planning and recording.

53. Teachers and nursery nurses work closely together throughout the day. At the beginning and end of each session they are on hand to welcome parents and their children, to exchange information with them, to listen, to reassure and to discuss children's progress. As children settle into their daily routine, two broad types of activity may be distinguished: those chosen by children from the range available, such as exploratory play with magnets or imaginative role play, and those activities initiated by adults; for example, singing or sorting and discussing simple three-dimensional shapes.

54. When children are engaged on their self-chosen tasks, the teacher and nursery assistant share their attention among the groups of children. On one occasion, for example, the teacher worked with a small group in the classroom shop extending children's early mathematical experience; she then helped another group to observe and experiment with objects in a science display to do with sound. The nursery assistant concentrated on children gathered around the water tray but also attended to others who were painting pictures and constructing models from scrap materials. Her support ranged from ensuring that children wore protective aprons to extending children's spoken language through discussion by encouraging them to describe, explain and predict. Meanwhile, the part-time nursery assistant joined a group of children playing at hospitals. Acting as a patient she helped pupils to explore the roles of nurses and doctors and to understand what goes on in hospitals. She introduced the beginnings of writing by encouraging the 'doctors' to write their marks on a prescription pad from left to right. At these times the teacher and the nursery assistants were constantly aware of the whole class and the pattern of adult interaction with both groups and individuals. The nursery assistant who has a special interest in art and craft gave considerable attention to children who chose these kinds of activity.

55.   Support from the nursery assistant helps the teacher to group the children flexibly for a variety of purposes. Thus, the nursery assistant may tell a story to most of the class while the teacher gives special attention to a small group. At other times three groups may be formed, each with an adult, to discuss some work the children have done; or the nursery assistant may extract a small group for cookery in the kitchen. Support from the nursery assistant is invaluable in outdoor play where some activities, such as the use of climbing frames, need careful supervision for safety.   In all these activities the nursery assistant actively supports children's learning and encourages progress in the directions planned by the teacher. The children benefit from much more individual attention than could be provided by the teacher alone.

56.   The nursery classrooms are constantly serviced by the assistants, who keep them tidy and help to ensure that equipment is used efficiently.   This involves, for example, fixing paper to painting easels, mopping-up around water trays, and returning to the hanging-rail dressing-up clothes used by children for role play.   There has to be a continuous process if equipment used by one group of children is to be ready for the next.   Such tasks are not delegated wholly to the nursery assistants but are shared by all adults.   They are seen in the context of children's personal and social development as an opportunity to teach consideration for one another and care for the surroundings.   From the beginning children are taught to choose the equipment they want, to replace it afterwards, and to help adults to tidy up as necessary.   The nursery assistants play an important part in this process.   In addition they contribute greatly to the smooth running of the nursery by attending sympathetically and speedily to children's personal needs, whether it is helping to change shoes or to administer simple first-aid.   This frees the teachers to concentrate on teaching.

57.   As the role of the nursery assistants has expanded, so has their concern to further their own professional development. Since very little in-service training is available locally for nursery assistants, the school has devised its own.   This includes involvement of the nursery assistants in school-based in-service training provided for the whole staff, arranging for them to visit and observe work in other schools, and voluntary membership of a local association concerned with the education of young children.

The primary school secretary

58.   It is Monday morning at five past nine; the telephone rings and the school secretary answers. She makes an appointment for a new parent to see the head on Thursday morning. Later in the morning a delivery van arrives. The secretary checks the delivery of parcels, signs receipts, unpacks the materials, enters them in the stock book and stores them in their allotted places. The head continues to teach her class uninterrupted. If this had been the afternoon the head would have had to leave her class to deal with both the telephone and the delivery van, for this is a village school with a teaching head and a part-time secretary.

59.   There are 39 children on roll aged 4–11 years. A full-time teacher is responsible for the infant class and the head teaches the juniors. A part-time teacher releases the head for one day a week for administration and for a further half day a week to allow the head to give extra attention to a child with special educational needs.

60.   The head is conscious of a considerable increase in general administrative and clerical work over the past few years, much of it associated with the implementation of the Education

Reform Act, particularly the introduction of the National Curriculum and the gradual devolution of funding to schools. She tries to ensure that administration of these changes does not interfere too much with her main tasks of teaching a class and managing the school. About two years before the inspection the head had recognised that the emerging demands of financial administration could not be contained within the 10 hours a week allocated for the school secretary. She therefore persuaded the school governors to employ a financial assistant for two hours a week, paid out of the school's own funds. They were able to appoint an exceptionally well qualified candidate; an honours graduate with secretarial qualifications, a good knowledge of computing and substantial experience in local government administration. She lives in the village and her children attended the school. The former secretary has now left the school and the financial assistant has taken on both roles. Recently the LEA had allocated the school an extra five hours a week for financial administration and as a result the school secretary is now employed for 15 hours a week; however, she finds that this is not enough and regularly puts in about half as much time again, voluntarily. A recent job description provided by the LEA for school secretaries listed her main duties and responsibilities as follows:

- to use new technology to undertake ordering and invoicing, including coding and checking off against computer print-outs as appropriate

- to maintain up-to-date financial records covering commitments and expenditure, and to prepare estimates for submission to head and governors

- to collate, order and distribute consortium orders

- to act as clerk to the governing body, including arranging meetings, preparing agendas, minutes and reports and dealing with any necessary correspondence

- to arrange lettings for the use of the school by outside bodies, ensuring the collection and payment of appropriate fees

- to assist the head teacher to monitor the upkeep of the premises and grounds, ensuring the necessary maintenance is arranged as appropriate

- to assist in the control of expenditure including petty cash, by the maintenance of records, and assisting with ordering and invoicing for goods

- to maintain diaries, make appointments and travel arrangements, including the booking of coaches as necessary

- to maintain inventories of school equipment for insurance purposes

- to undertake any other appropriate duties as required for the efficient running of the school office.

61.   The secretary is in school for half of every day during term time. She shares with the head a small office which was created during improvements to the old building and which is situated conveniently near the main entrance. It provides the usual office equipment and a computer which was bought out of school funds. She perceives her function as undertaking all routine administration so that the head is free to concentrate on making managerial decisions and on her professional role in teaching, curriculum planning and staff development.

62.   The bulk of the secretary's work is evenly split between finance and general administration. She also acts as reception-

ist and telephonist, and occasionally assists with the acquisition and preparation of teaching materials; for example, arranging to borrow books for topic work from the schools library service. She is clerk to the school governors and secretary to the local small schools group.

63. There is a fairly regular pattern to the week's work. On Monday mornings she receives money brought by children for school dinners, and takes contributions to the school fund which is used to support swimming tuition and educational visits, to buy ingredients for cookery lessons, for donations to charities and for purchase of books. From time to time there is substantial income from parental fund-raising events. The secretary collects the money from classrooms, checks it, enters it into the appropriate account and takes it to the bank (a five-mile round trip). Such work does not stop at accounting but includes, for example, liaison with the school kitchen and regular checks on meals received and paid for by individual children. The amount passing through the school fund in a year varies between £8,000 and £12,000. The secretary monitors interest earned and discusses with the head and governors where funds should be placed to best advantage.

64. The head and the governors annually allocate delegated funds under a number of headings such as minor building repairs, heating and teaching materials. Directed by the head, the secretary places orders and constantly monitors expenditure against targets most efficiently. She has introduced standard accounting procedures which meet the requirements of the LEA auditors, and prepares a termly breakdown of expenditure under each heading for a meeting of the governors' financial sub-committee which is attended by the head. This information speeds up decision-making and helps the committee to forecast expenditure more accurately, to monitor expenditure and to make adjustments as necessary. The secre-

tary has introduced and developed computer systems to support these administrative tasks. She and the head had been greatly encouraged, at a day's training provided by the LEA on LMS a short time before HMI's visit, to find that the system they had already developed could be made compatible with one about to be recommended by the LEA.

65.   While the school decides how its delegated funds should be spent, accounts are still paid by the LEA. Consequently, the secretary devotes a good deal of her time to making out orders, certifying that goods have been received and work carried out, and reconciling her accounts with payment records from the LEA computer.

66.   The school secretary's routine administrative and clerical duties include maintaining pupils' records; typing, reproducing and distributing information for parents; typing and compiling school brochures, policy statements and other curricular documents; filing and maintaining stock control and inventories. Correspondence from the LEA arrives by courier twice a week; she sorts letters, drafts replies for the head's approval, completes routine statistical returns and answers enquiries. The head makes decisions about educational visits, supply cover for teacher absence and the school-based in-service training to be undertaken. The secretary then saves the head's time by making many of the arrangements and keeping records and accounts.

67.   There is a constant need for the school to liaise with parents, suppliers, maintenance contractors and the LEA over matters ranging from educational visits to building repairs. Much of this time-consuming work is done efficiently by the secretary on behalf of the head. She also takes up personnel matters with the LEA on behalf of teachers.

68. For most of the time the secretary works on her own, guided by consultations with the head twice a day. On one day a week the head does not teach but spends the morning on administrative tasks, dealing with correspondence and returns prepared by the secretary, amending typed drafts, meeting parents and others by appointment, and planning for the staff meeting held at the end of the day. In the afternoon the secretary joins her to consider the school diary and the schedule of tasks which support the management of the school. They review progress in the past week and set targets for the week ahead. The head emphasises the importance of these meetings in ensuring that the secretary is well informed and able to respond to many demands without having to interrupt the head in the classroom.

69. As clerk to the school governors, the secretary prepares agendas for meetings, writes minutes and handles correspondence. Attendance at meetings reinforces her understanding of school policies which affect her work as school secretary.

70. This school gains enormously from the services of its efficient secretary whose skills are fully used. As a telephonist and receptionist she helps to maintain good communications with parents and the wider community while shielding the head from constant interruptions to her teaching. The secretary's administrative and clerical work saves the head's time and assists the smooth running of the school. The head is speedily alerted to any potential problems so that decisions can be taken quickly about any necessary action. The secretary's financial skills provide head and governors with clear and up-to-date information which helps them to make good management decisions and to monitor and control expenditure effectively. The secretary reminds the head of events in the school diary so that the head has ample time to prepare for important meetings and to brief the secretary about any papers to be

prepared. Considerable administrative responsibility has been wisely delegated to the secretary. The head ensures that the secretary is familiar with school policies and practices within which to exercise her responsibilities.

Classroom ancillaries in a primary school

71.   No one starts out as a paid classroom ancillary in this school.   All begin as voluntary helpers who are carefully inducted into the job. The result is ancillary help of unusually high quality which effectively supports both teaching and learning.

72.   The school has 160 children aged 5 to 9 years.   These include 17 pupils who have general learning difficulties and who are based in a special unit but integrated into the mainstream classes for much of their work.   The teaching staff consists of the head and eight teachers, two of whom are responsible for the children in the special unit.   The school is situated in a small town.   It mainly serves a private estate of small houses which has developed rapidly over the last ten years. Some of the parents are self-employed while others have skilled and semi-skilled jobs; there are no professional parents. About a fifth of the children come from a local authority housing estate. The children who attend the special unit are drawn from the whole of the surrounding area.

73.   The head gives high priority to maintaining a close partnership with parents built up since the school opened (a period of eight years at the time of HMI's visit); this includes encouraging them to give voluntary assistance in school.   At termly meetings for the parents of children who have just started school the head explains the workings of the school and invites parents to volunteer their services, an appeal supported by

reminders in regular news sheets which draw attention to the various ways in which help can be given. From time to time special requests are made for extra assistance with events such as educational visits and the school fair. General appeals are supplemented by personal invitations to parents who begin to show an interest and to those who have particular skills to offer, such as needlecraft. Often existing helpers persuade others to join.

74. Voluntary classroom assistants help in a variety of ways; for example, they assist with swimming, help children to change library books, oversee small groups and guide children in the use of the school's computers. Before they start working in school, the head gives all volunteers an introductory talk about their role. She explains how they will be guided by the teachers and emphasises the importance of building up good relationships with the children, projecting attitudes consistent with the school ethos, and respecting the confidentiality of personal information they may acquire. After their first experience of working in the school, parents meet the head again to discuss their impressions, raise questions and consider the tasks they might perform regularly. As tasks are identified, the head talks individually with each voluntary classroom assistant about the educational purpose of the activity he or she will help to supervise.

75. The teacher to whom the voluntary assistant is assigned begins by giving the helper detailed instructions about one activity to be supervised; she explains its educational purposes and what the children are expected to get out of it. The teacher then guides the helper in organising the activity and provides notes. Voluntary assistants learn on the job by carrying out their set tasks, and by observing teachers at work. The head and teachers constantly monitor the volunteers and get to know the interests, strengths and skills of each parent. A few parents

are happiest with tasks such as preparing materials for the teacher, while others make their best contribution supporting the work of small groups of children.

76.   The head provides regular training in the form of one-hour sessions twice a term for all classroom assistants, both voluntary and paid.   At these times she talks about a topic such as handwriting, children's language development, or control and discipline.   She explains school policies, purposes and practices and this is followed by discussion.

77.   Vacancies for paid ancillary staff are filled by voluntary helpers whose capabilities are already known.   The first step is usually to become one of the eight paid mid-day supervisory assistants.   They work for six-and-a-quarter hours a week, spending five hours on lunchtime supervision and one-and-a-quarter hours on general classroom assistance.   Most give the general classroom assistance as a single session once a week but some, with the teachers' agreement, split it into two shorter periods.

78.   This arrangement has enhanced the status of the supervisory assistants and given them greater variety and job satisfaction.   Working under the direction of a teacher improves their techniques for managing the children, reduces the teacher's workload and enriches children's experience.   Seeing the same children at work in the classroom as during lunch times and recreation helps to give them a deeper understanding of the children and better opportunities to build positive relationships.   This strategy has benefited both children's work in the classrooms and the quality of midday supervision.

79.   There are five paid classroom ancillaries, who originally started as voluntary helpers and have been carefully chosen and trained for their current work.   One has general duties and

the others help the children with special needs. They are deployed flexibly to meet the changing needs of children in the various classes. In 1989–90, for example, the general ancillary shared her time (12 hours a week) among three classes, but at the time of HMI's visit was spending all her time with the reception class where the teacher was new and there were several children in need of extra support. One special needs ancillary works in the special unit but, since the children are taught mostly in mainstream classes, she concentrates her efforts where support is most needed and at the time of the visit this was in Year 1. The other three special needs ancillaries each support individual children with special educational needs, both alongside the teachers in ordinary classrooms and in the special unit. One works for $18^{1}/_{4}$ hours and two for 25 hours.

80. The ancillaries spend considerable time working with small groups of children, but decisions about deployment are made by the class teacher on the basis of the work to be done by the children and the nature of support required. Sometimes the teacher concentrates on intensive teaching with a small group while the ancillary oversees the rest of the class working on activities arranged by the teacher. In all cases the teacher plans and prepares work to be undertaken by the children and then briefs the ancillary about activities to be supervised, explaining their educational purposes. The ancillary notes the main points in her personal record book, but the amount of detail depends on her previous knowledge and experience of the activity. As the children work she notes their individual achievements and difficulties in her record book for discussion with the teacher later in the day. The following examples seen by HMI give some impression of the ancillaries at work.

81. The teacher of the reception class organised a number of learning activities for small groups: imaginative role play, number recognition games and the beginnings of counting,

making picture stories, an introduction to operating a computer and sharing library books with an adult. She was assisted by a general and a special ancillary and by a voluntary helper who does library duties. All three had been briefed about their contribution to the afternoon's work.

82. The general ancillary withdrew two children to a reading area which was shared with other classes and where computers were set up. Normally she would have had six children, but two of the three computers were temporarily out of use. She taught the children to play a computer game and introduced them to simple commands. They learned to use particular keys such as the space bar, and followed a simple diagram which she had drawn, gaining confidence in using the keyboard and in giving commands. The ancillary had excellent relationships with the children: she praised and reassured while encouraging them to think for themselves, to predict and to try out their own ideas. The children were learning to share, to take turns and to co-operate, as well as developing appropriate skills. The activity completed, the ancillary noted the children's responses and withdrew two more from the class. In this way she gradually covered the whole class.

83. Within the classroom, the special needs ancillary introduced a physically handicapped child to her task of sorting, matching and grouping a selection of objects. After checking that the child had understood and could manage on her own, the ancillary turned to a small group of children at the same table. They were drawing sequences of pictures to tell a story about a windy day and the ancillary sympathetically discussed their ideas, skilfully using questions to help them recall experiences earlier in the week when they worked with the teacher on this topic. As the children finished their pictures they dictated captions which the ancillary wrote under the pictures. She encouraged the children to use skills they already possessed

such as writing their own name alongside the title of the story. She constantly kept an eye on her special charge and attended to her needs as necessary.

84. In the cosy library corner a voluntary helper, who was also a parent and governor, sat with a child who had just chosen a library book to take home for his parents to read to him. The helper read part of the story and they discussed events and identified people in the illustrations. She checked his understanding of the text and of individual words by asking questions and inviting comments. She occasionally drew attention to features of the language such as an illustration with a capital A and the same letter used elsewhere in lower case. Satisfied, she noted down the title of the book he had chosen and a comment and turned to another child. This ancillary also worked with older classes where children are helped to select two books, one from a colour coded range which they can read for themselves and another from the library shelves to read with their parents. The quality of interaction was high, the adult's reading clear and sensitive. She encouraged the children to search for meaning in the print, and encouraged and respected their personal responses.

85. The carefully planned use of these three ancillaries relieved pressure on the class teacher and allowed her to concentrate her professional skills on two groups of children for the whole of this session. The children undoubtedly benefited from the extra attention.

86. In a neighbouring classroom of older children, the special needs ancillary cared for two children with considerable language difficulties. The speech therapist visits once a week to work with these children; she discusses their progress with the class teacher and the ancillary and gives advice. As a result the teacher modifies the children's programme of work and ex-

plains what is required to the ancillary, who helps to implement the programme by working with the children, and by overseeing the remainder of the class for short periods while the teacher concentrates on these two children on their own or as part of a larger group.

87.   The planned use of classroom ancillaries carefully trained to work under the teachers' close supervision brings many benefits to the teaching and learning in this school. It also brings rewards for the ancillaries themselves by expanding their understanding of children and their development: this gives them a sense of achievement and increased self-esteem. For a few it acts as a valuable stepping-stone to employment or re-employment in schools and in the wider community.

Secondary science technicians

88.   This is a large secondary school, with around 1,500 pupils aged 11–18 years, including a sixth form of 400. The head of the science department insisted, 'We simply could not do our job without the support we receive from our technicians. Science in the National Curriculum is a practical subject and effective teaching depends on having the right equipment and materials in place for each lesson; and knowing you can rely on it.' Preparing and maintaining resources for science is a massive and time-consuming task which takes place quickly and efficiently out of sight of the busy classrooms. Confident in the quality of support they receive, teachers are able to concentrate on tasks which demand their special skills: curriculum development, lesson planning, teaching, meeting pupils' individual needs, marking pupils' work, assessing and recording progress.

89.   The school's nine laboratories are no longer sufficient for the growing number of pupils and about a quarter of the lessons

have to be taught in ordinary classrooms. Good servicing allows laboratories to be used intensively and they are regularly occupied for 93 per cent of teaching time.

90. The carefully chosen team consists of a senior science technician and three science technicians. All have suitable training and qualifications such as a BTEC diploma, and all have a career commitment to laboratory work. Their skills and interests complement one another. The senior science technician specialises in resources for physical science, two technicians oversee resources for chemistry and biology respectively, while the third technician covers the broad spectrum of resources for an integrated science course with younger pupils. Their range of experience extends from the senior science technician with over 30 years in laboratory work to a newcomer trained at the local college of further education. All are employed full-time ($37\frac{1}{2}$ hours a week) though one does not work during school holidays.

91. The technicians work as a team but, as in many other schools, this is not helped by a building where small preparation rooms are scattered throughout the science department. Each is responsible for his own preparation room, for maintaining its tidiness, security and resources. The senior technician has a small office and a workshop with a workbench and tools.

92. The senior science technician is the line manager for the other technicians and is responsible for their deployment, support, training and supervision. He is answerable to the head of the science department and attends all meetings of the department. During their first month in the school, new science technicians are inducted into the work of the department. They work alongside the senior technician, receiving advice from him on setting up and operating complex equipment and learning departmental routines. He is always available to give

advice. When new equipment and procedures are introduced, he explains and demonstrates them to the whole team and emphasises safety aspects. At the time of HMI's visit he was building up on computer information about advanced experiments and procedures regularly used. This information lists the equipment and materials needed and gives advice on setting-up and operation, thus providing a source of speedy reference for science teachers and the other technicians.

93. In addition to this school-focussed training technicians are encouraged to join a technicians' group which was set up by the LEA, about three years before HMI's visit, to provide mutual support and training. Training days have addressed such topics as the storage and stock control of chemicals and the maintenance of microscopes. Members receive bulletins, newsletters and an advice service from a university-based schools science service.

94. The resources required for each science lesson are set out on a simple proforma by the teacher for the senior technician, at least 24 hours before the class, so that he can allocate the work to his team. Equipment for the co-ordinated science course in Years 10 and 11 and for sixth form science is categorised under biology, chemistry or physics. It is usually serviced by the appropriate technician from his preparation room, with some inter-change depending on volume of work. The technician servicing the lower school science often has to provide a wide variety of material for as many as 21 lessons a day and is supported as necessary by the others.

95. Technicians prepare materials and equipment to the teachers' specifications and deliver them by the stated time to the appropriate laboratory by trolley. Some of this preparation is skilled work, especially for the older classes, where for example precise volumetric solutions are made up for work in chemistry.

Particular care is needed in preparing material for A-level practical examinations. At the end of each lesson used equipment is removed, checked, cleaned and serviced with particular attention given to its safety. Pressure of work means that some maintenance has to be delayed until late in the day and during school holidays.

96. The senior technician constantly monitors the state of preparation rooms, condition of equipment and quality of service given to teachers. Every opportunity is taken to reduce the amount of unskilled work done by technicians in order to make full use of their knowledge and skills. Shortly before the HMI visit, for example, the school had decided to invest in a heavy-duty dishwasher adapted to take scientific equipment such as test tubes, thereby reducing time spent on washing glassware.

97. The senior technician in this school has a sound knowledge of computers and a high level of skills in engineering, glass-blowing and photography, attributes which are used profitably in a number of ways. Within guidelines set by the head of science, he maintains stock control and is responsible for ordering, receiving and storing materials, including first-aid supplies, textbooks and stationery. This is achieved efficiently through the use of a microcomputer programmed to show levels of stock this highlights items which are running low and prints orders to designated suppliers on command. The senior technician also helps the head of science to prepare the annual budget and keeps departmental accounts. These are computerised and teaching staff responsible for the different science subjects are each given a monthly statement of account. These systems save the teachers' time, enabling them to maintain close control of expenditure and to make informed decisions about spending. When expensive new equipment is needed the senior technician helps the science department to obtain good value for money,

investigating available alternatives, assessing their quality and making recommendations to the teachers.

98. The senior technician saves the head of department's time by arranging for contractors to deal with breakdowns of plant and by negotiating contracts for major items of equipment such as fume cupboards. All such work is carefully checked upon completion.

99. By repairing, making and improving equipment the senior technician reduces departmental costs and gives strong support to teachers engaged in curriculum development. For example, the head of science was introducing new work in biotechnology: he had produced specifications for a fermentation unit with computer monitoring and the senior technician had built the equipment at low cost and set it up. Sometimes teachers want to introduce new equipment and techniques which could improve their work but find it difficult to get time to try these out. On request, the senior technician will test them and give advice on their performance and use.

100. The senior technician's interest in photography is put to good use for examination purposes in recording the children's project work in science and in other subjects such as design technology. He also makes sets of colour slides commissioned by teachers.

101. The head of science is responsible for safety in the science department but the senior technician also monitors procedures and scans safety bulletins received from the LEA and other sources. He draws teachers' attention to action which needs to be taken, displays new information on the departmental notice-board and enters a copy into the safety file. The head regularly consults him about safety in relation to equipment in other parts of the school.

102. The science teachers make considerable use of microcomputers, which the senior technician sets up along with interfacing equipment. Occasionally, when new and expensive equipment is being brought into use, he works in laboratories alongside teachers and assists them as well as the pupils to use it effectively. As a result such equipment rarely suffers damage from incorrect handling.

103. Although the senior technician's major responsibility is to the science department, his services are used throughout the school. He oversees the use of all audiovisual equipment, gives advice on types of equipment to buy and carries out most of the servicing and repairs. This results in high reliability while economising on costs. His responsibilities extend to recording video material off air, editing tapes, searching tapes for the part required in particular lessons and delivering trolley-mounted television and video recorder sets, ready to play, to the appropriate teaching area. He also sets up audiovisual services for meetings held in the school, such as public meetings and in-service training courses.

104. The school has two general technicians who further extend the pool of technical skills. One is a former teacher qualified in craft, design and technology; the other, who holds an Ordinary National Certificate, has a developing interest in computers and information technology generally. The senior science technician is responsible for the administration, management and effectiveness of their work. Heads of department make requests to him for particular projects which they are able to fund out of their budgets; he then allocates work to the technician best equipped to do it, taking account of available time, costs and the priorities expressed by each department. Individual projects are designed, planned and costed by technicians to meet specifications set out by subject departments. Recent projects at the time of HMI's visit ranged from cataloguing

specimens for the geology department to building secure storage units for musical instruments. At quieter times and during school holidays a few larger projects had been undertaken such as converting cloakrooms into secure storage areas for science resources, and building an architect-designed and LEA-approved partition in the design technology area. Several projects which would otherwise have been too expensive to contemplate had been completed in this way.

Non-teaching staff in a secondary school

105. The school is situated on the outskirts of the town. There are nearly 1,000 pupils aged 11–18, and a teaching staff of 60 together with 18 non-teaching staff and four midday supervisors. The head and bursar, who arrived at the school on the same day in 1983, found the school well staffed but most non-teaching staff were scattered across the school working for individual departments. The service was fragmented and uneven and as a consequence some departments were well supported while others had too little help. Working closely with the bursar and senior staff, the head set out to provide coherent and unified non-teaching support for the whole school. This was intended to increase the effectiveness of the staff as a whole and to give greater job satisfaction.

106. Teachers were consulted about whether more support was needed. The bursar analysed responses, examined the work undertaken by non-teaching staff and drew up a list of responsibilities which could be assumed by them under her leadership. These ranged from providing secretarial and reprographic services to administering the school's finances and overseeing the maintenance of the fabric and furnishings. The senior management team agreed a plan for gradual change.

107. As a first step all the secretarial staff were brought into a central secretariat based on the school office and charged with providing a fast administration service of high quality. Requests for their services are made on a standard proforma and handed to the school secretary. Two clerks are responsible directly to the bursar, administering many of the school's finances, collecting money, writing cheques and recording transactions.

108. A central reprographics service conveniently adjoins the staff room. Services offered by a full-time technician include copying, printing and graphics together with audio and video recording, and handling bookings for audiovisual hardware. The reprographics service is self-financing through charges to departmental budgets. The centralisation of this service has enabled the school to improve significantly the quality of reprographics equipment.

109. The reorganisation was accompanied by measures to improve working conditions. The staff room, used by all, was carpeted and a workroom added; the office was carpeted and refurnished and the kitchen modernised. A new telephone system saves time and eases communication within and between the scattered buildings, and gives direct access to outside lines for those who need it, such as the matron and the careers teacher. Increasing the number of outside lines has pleased the parents and others in the community who had found it frustrating trying to get through to the school at busy times.

110. Some changes in the deployment of non-teaching staff were associated with changes in the school curriculum and in educational practice. Remedial work, for example, used to be carried out by three teachers who each gave a small part of their time to withdrawing children from ordinary classes for concentrated remedial teaching. The school decided to provide reme-

dial support within ordinary lessons and the subsequent depar-
ture of the three teachers facilitated a change in the arrangements. Remedial support is now provided in classrooms by a
full-time specialist teacher assisted by two welfare assistants.
Funding for this change came from the LEA's provision of
ancillary support for children with special educational needs,
topped-up from the school's own staffing budget.

111. The roles of technicians were also changing as design
technology took shape within the curriculum. The home eco-
nomics technician, for example, was spending less time servicing this subject and giving more general assistance in art,
design technology and the maintenance of other areas such as
physical education equipment. A science technician was giving
some of her time to specialist work in the design technology
department. Within the science department a review of the
technician service instigated by the bursar had increased
efficiency. The teachers had a new pro-forma system for
ordering lesson materials well in advance, and storage systems
for printed material had been improved.

112. Benefits had been gained by adjusting the balance of work
between teachers and non-teaching staff. When the examinations officer (a teacher with a scale B allowance) retired, it was
found that a good deal of the routine administration could be
done by non-teaching support, and the duties were shared
between a teacher (scale A), who deals with examination
entries and queries from all departments, and the school
matron, who provides administrative support for the teacher.
Freed from most of the paper-work and time-consuming telephone calls to examination boards, the teacher spends more
time teaching than his predecessor, and the matron puts to
good use time during the week when her nursing skills are not
in demand.

113. The bursar's role evolved in parallel with these changes. She started as office manager and keeper of the school accounts, but working closely with the head and deputy she gradually assumed responsibility for managing the school's administration. When the post was up-graded in 1989 she was made a full member of the senior management group and, along with deputy heads and senior teachers, she reports directly to the head. She ensures that the school's communications and administrative systems are effective. The school secretary assumed the role of office manager and the bursar's main activities are now as follows:

i. Overseeing the work of all non-teaching staff. This includes recruitment, management, training, supervision by monitoring and reviewing workloads and standards, assessing future staffing needs, counselling non-teaching staff, and staffing special projects. Within this structure heads of subject departments oversee within their departments the day-to-day work of non-teaching staff such as technicians and welfare assistants (classroom ancillaries).

ii. Ensuring good communications within the school. This includes advising all staff on matters such as school management and administrative procedures, legislation, budgeting, salaries and job descriptions, offering careers advice, and ensuring that there is an effective flow of information between staff at all levels.

iii. As a member of the senior management group:

- overseeing the control and monitoring of resources, material and financial

- generating resources, for example by seeking sponsorships from industry and commerce, and setting up trust funds

- extending and maintaining links with the community, press and media; marketing to the community the school's resources both educational and physical; overseeing the environmental needs and maintenance of the site and buildings

- identifying activities which are carried out by teachers but which might be performed appropriately by other staff, thus giving the teachers more time to concentrate on their teaching.

114. All these activities are undertaken in close consultation at weekly meetings with the head and other members of the senior management group: a deputy head, two senior teachers and the bursar. The bursar helps to ensure that the group is efficiently serviced, its decisions are rapidly communicated and any necessary administrative action is quickly taken. The bursar also attends weekly meetings of the finance and resources group which allocates resources, monitors the budget and provides heads of department with regular balance sheets. These meetings, together with those of the school policy group, made up of the head, four governors, senior staff and the bursar, provide guidelines within which the bursar administers the school funds.

115. The bursar's job is about working with people to promote efficiency and to get best value for money. There is a daily check with the school secretary on priorities and the secretariat's workload, and she spends considerable time on a wide range of matters such as discussing staff contracts with the LEA, advising teachers about new regulations for school journeys, checking sick-leave returns, arranging lettings and dealing with contractors over the maintenance of buildings and equipment. Sometimes she has to cope with the unexpected, for example, an accidental fire alarm or intruders. The job has a creative element which includes exploring ways of improving adminis-

tration and the service provided by non-teaching staff, and finding new ways of securing support from the local community.

116. As a full member of the senior management group, the bursar has a full knowledge of school policies and the authority to respond positively to many and varied demands. She helps to ensure the smooth running of the school and reduces pressure on the head and senior staff, enabling them to give greater attention to professional matters such as managing the curriculum, staff development and pastoral care.

POLYTECHNIC SOUTH WEST

ACADEMIC SERVICES

EDUCATION OBSERVED

NON-TEACHING STAFF IN SCHOOLS

A REVIEW BY HMI

HER MAJESTY'S INSPECTORATE
London: HMSO

© Crown copyright 1992
First published 1992
ISBN 0 11 270788 2

Designed and typeset by DES Information Branch
IB/1006/11/54

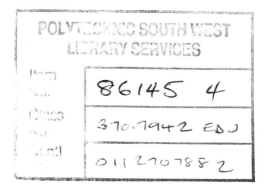